THE THIRD ANTI-COLORING BOOK

SUSAN STRIKER

Illustrated by
Susan Striker and
Edward Kimmel

With
Brent Brolin
Evelyn Osborne
Linda Gen

AN OWL BOOK / HENRY HOLT AND COMPANY / NEW YORK

To my son, Jason Scot Frederic Striker, for whom I have so many hopes and dreams, the most important of which is that he fulfill his own hopes and dreams rather than mine.

Henry Holt and Company, Inc.
Publishers since 1866
115 West 18th Street
New York, New York 10011

Henry Holt® is a registered trademark
of Henry Holt and Company, Inc.

Published in Canada by Fitzhenry & Whiteside Ltd.,
195 Allstate Parkway, Markham, Ontario L3R 4T8.

ISBN 0-8050-1447-0 (An Owl Book: pbk.)

Henry Holt books are available
for special promotions and premiums.
For details contact: Director, Special Markets.

Printed in the United States of America

10

Grateful acknowledgment is made to Lynne Mesznick and
to music copyist Christine Kissel.

The author and publisher wish to thank *Colloquy*
magazine for permission to reprint "About
School" from their January 1970 issue.

*"The creative spirit is a wild bird
that will not sing in captivity."*

—Van Dearing Perrine,
Let the Child Draw

Introduction

About School

He always wanted to say things. But no one understood.
He always wanted to explain things. But no one cared.
So he drew.

Sometimes he would just draw and it wasn't anything. He
    wanted to carve it in stone or write it in the sky.
He would lie out on the grass and look up in the sky and it would
    be only him and the sky and the things inside that needed
    saying.

And it was after that, that he drew the picture. It was a beautiful
    picture. He kept it under the pillow and would let no one
    see it.
And he would look at it every night and think about it. And when
    it was dark, and his eyes were closed, he could still see it.
And it was all of him. And he loved it.

When he started school he brought it with him. Not to show
    anyone, but just to have it with him like a friend.

It was funny about school.
He sat in a square, brown desk like all the other square, brown
    desks and he thought it should be red.
And his room was a square, brown room. Like all the other
    rooms.
And it was tight and close. And stiff.

He hated to hold the pencil and the chalk, with his arm stiff
    and his feet flat on the floor, with the teacher watching
    and watching.
And then he had to write numbers. And they weren't anything.
They were worse than the letters that could be something if you
    put them together.
And the numbers were tight and square and he hated the
    whole thing.

The teacher came and spoke to him. She told him to wear a tie
    like all the other boys. He said he didn't like them and she
    said it didn't matter.

After that they drew. And he drew all yellow and it was the way
he felt about morning. And it was beautiful.

The teacher came and smiled at him. "What's this?" she said.
"Why don't you draw something like Ken's drawing? Isn't
that beautiful?"
It was all questions.

After that his mother bought him a tie and he always drew
airplanes and rocket ships like everyone else.
And he threw the old picture away.
And when he lay out alone looking at the sky, it was big and
blue and all of everything, but he wasn't anymore.

He was square inside and brown, and his hands were stiff, and
he was like anyone else. And the thing inside him that
needed saying didn't need saying anymore.

It had stopped pushing. It was crushed. Stiff.
Like everything else.

—R. Nukerji

What is your earliest memory?

Can you guess what these children just found?

The king and queen live in
the grandest castle ever imagined.

You have been asked to design new playground equipment for the park.

When you say your prayers,
what do you pray for?

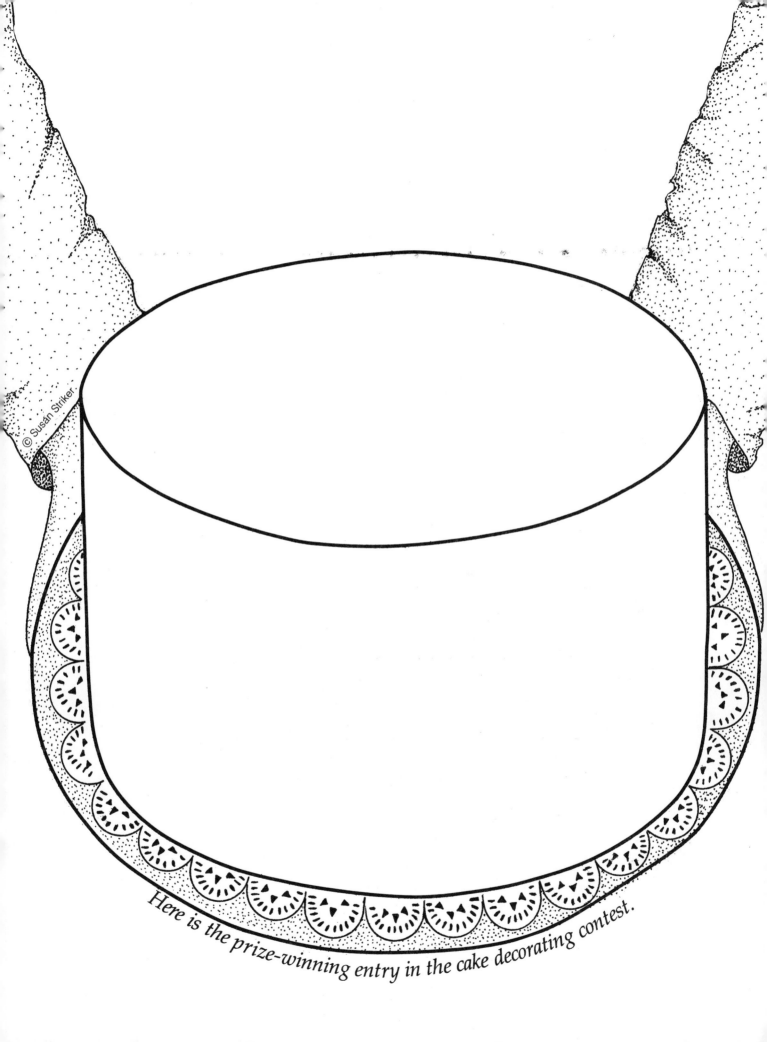

Here is the prize-winning entry in the cake decorating contest.

© Susán Striker·

Design costumes and scenery
for your favorite fairy tale.

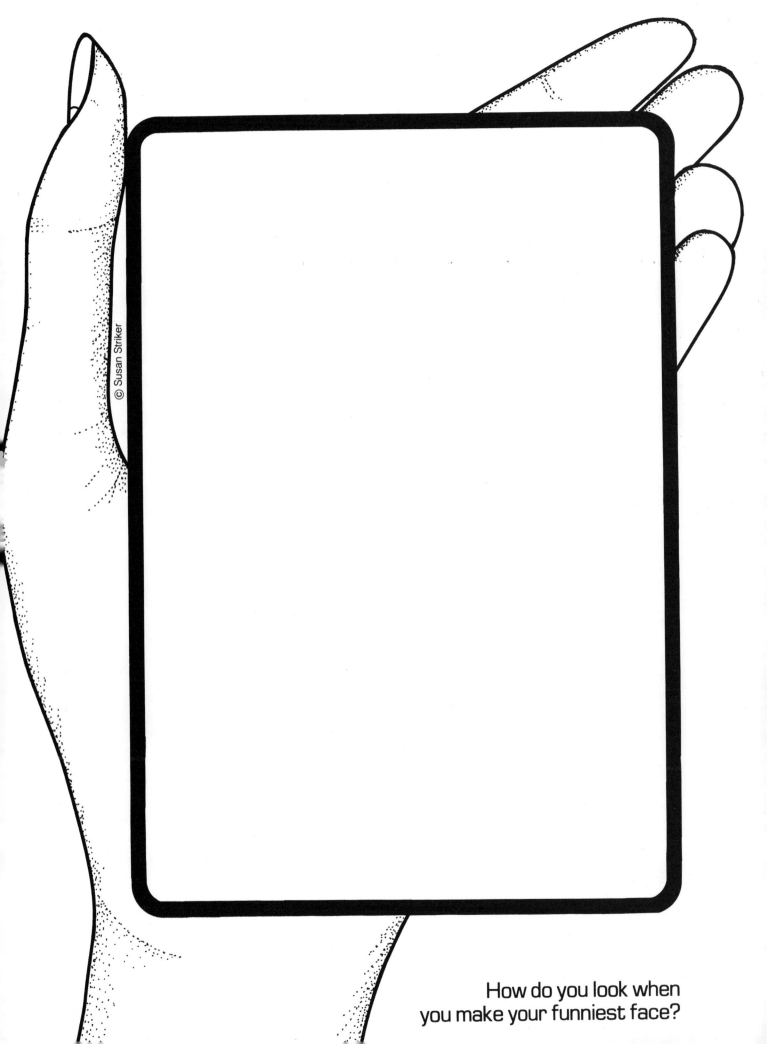

How do you look when
you make your funniest face?

When you hold a seashell up to your ear,
what do you think of?

© Susan Striker

What's the best idea you've ever had?

You have designed the
world's most spectacular
new pinball machine.

© Susan Striker

Did you ever stare
at the changing images
in a fire?

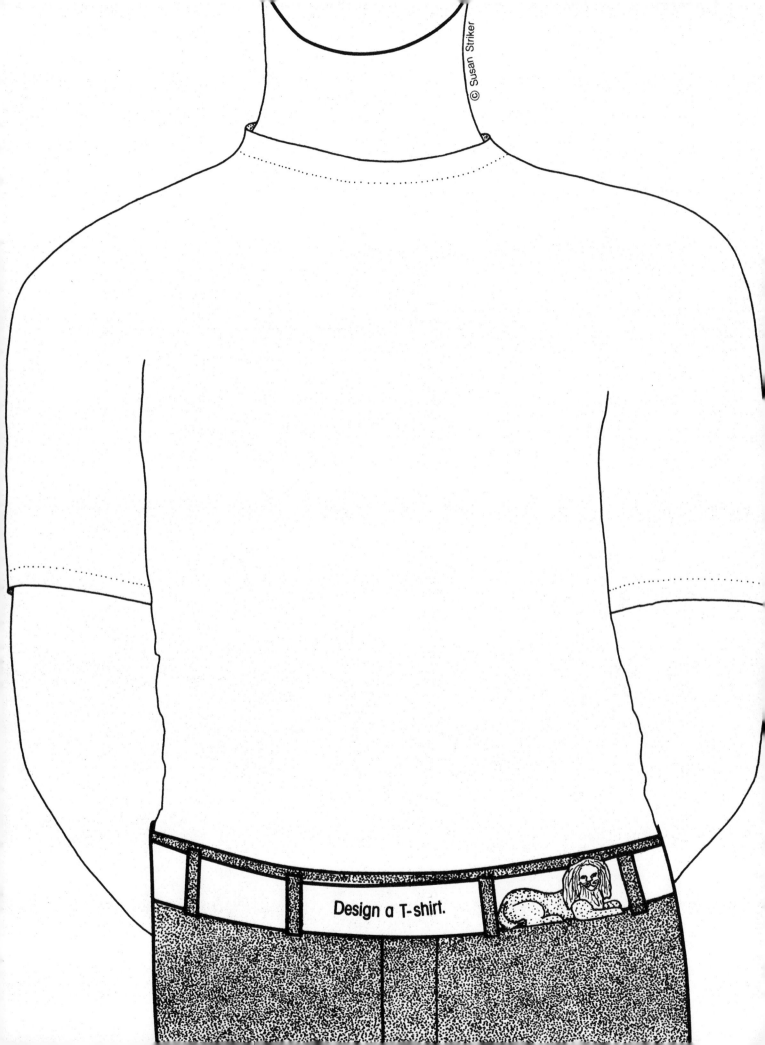

Design a T-shirt.

This is the key to _____.

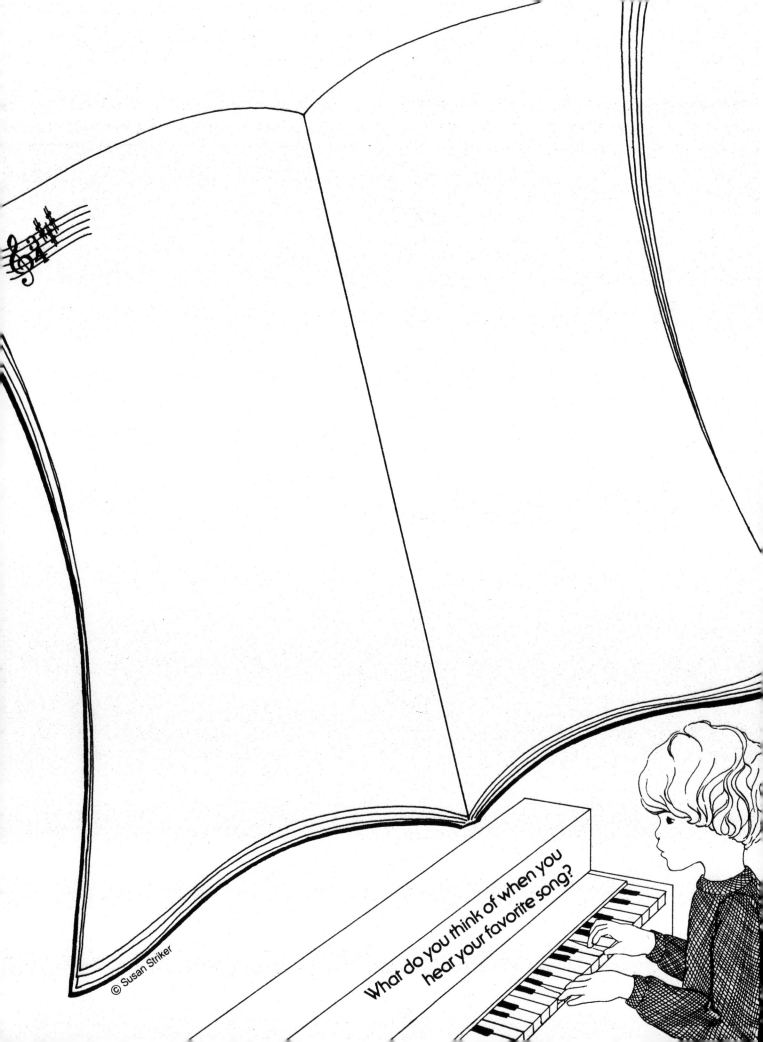

What do you think of when you hear your favorite song?

© Susan Striker

**Design a bumper sticker
to put on your car.**

© Susan Striker

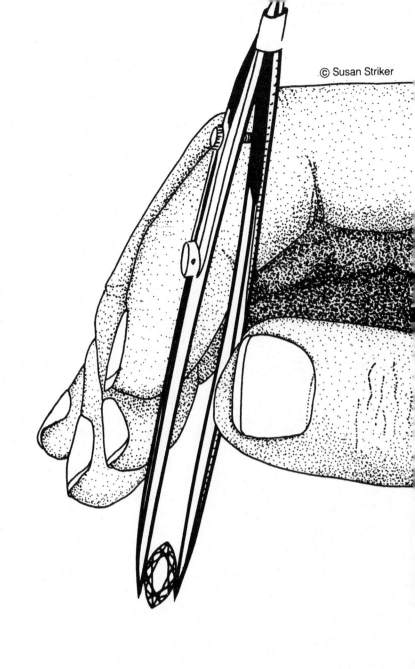

You are a talented jewelry designer.
The piece you are working on now is a gift for your mother.

What trick can this great magician do?

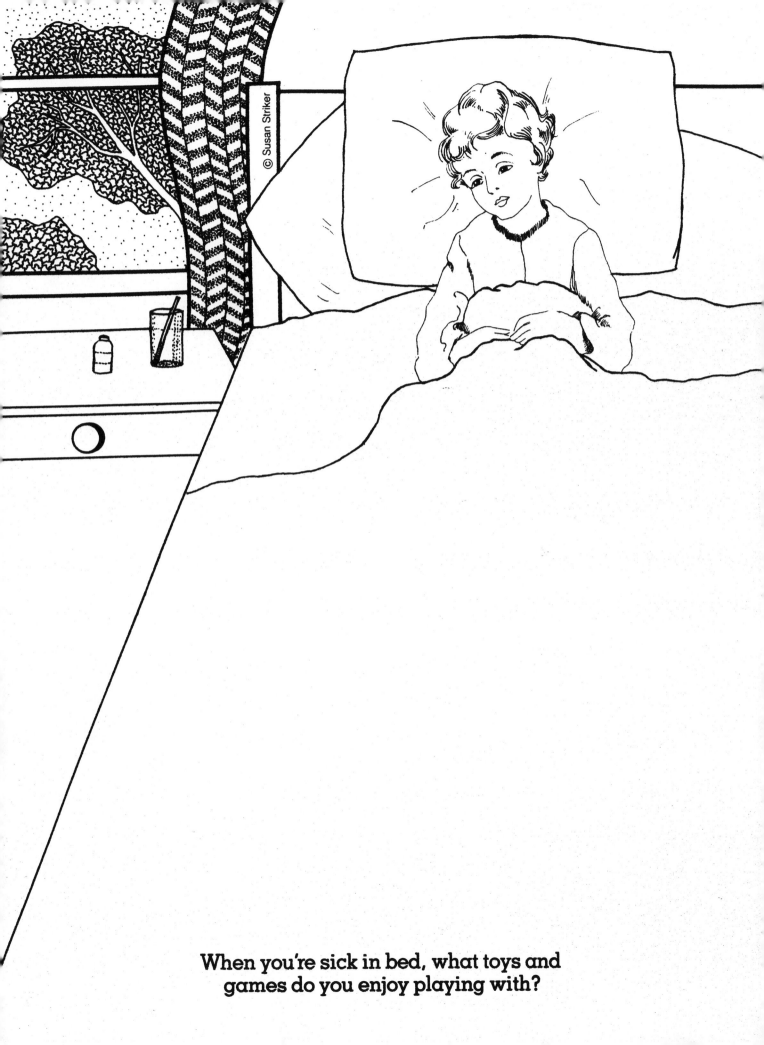

**When you're sick in bed, what toys and
games do you enjoy playing with?**

What poster will you
carry in the protest march?

© Susan Striker

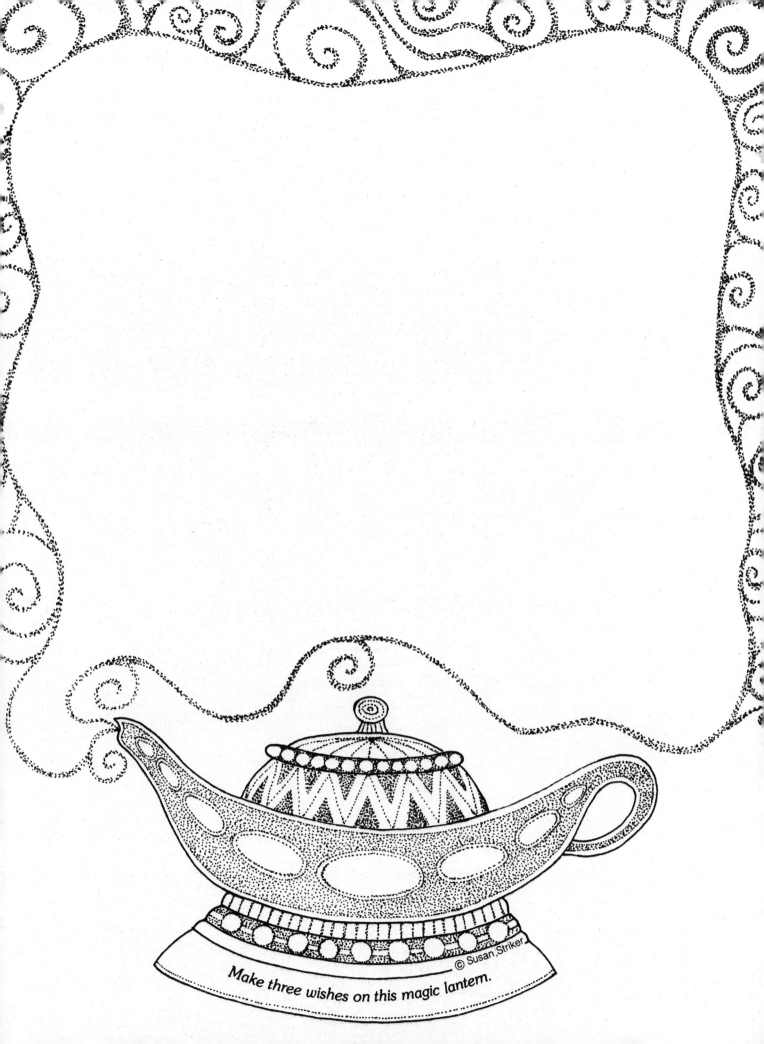

Make three wishes on this magic lantern.

© Susan Striker

© Susan Striker

You are secretary of the treasury
of a new nation. Design its money.

© Susan Striker

**Build a snowman and snowwoman, and dress
them in clothes your family has around the house.**

© Susan Striker

Archaeologists must reconstruct a prehistoric animal from these newly discovered bones.

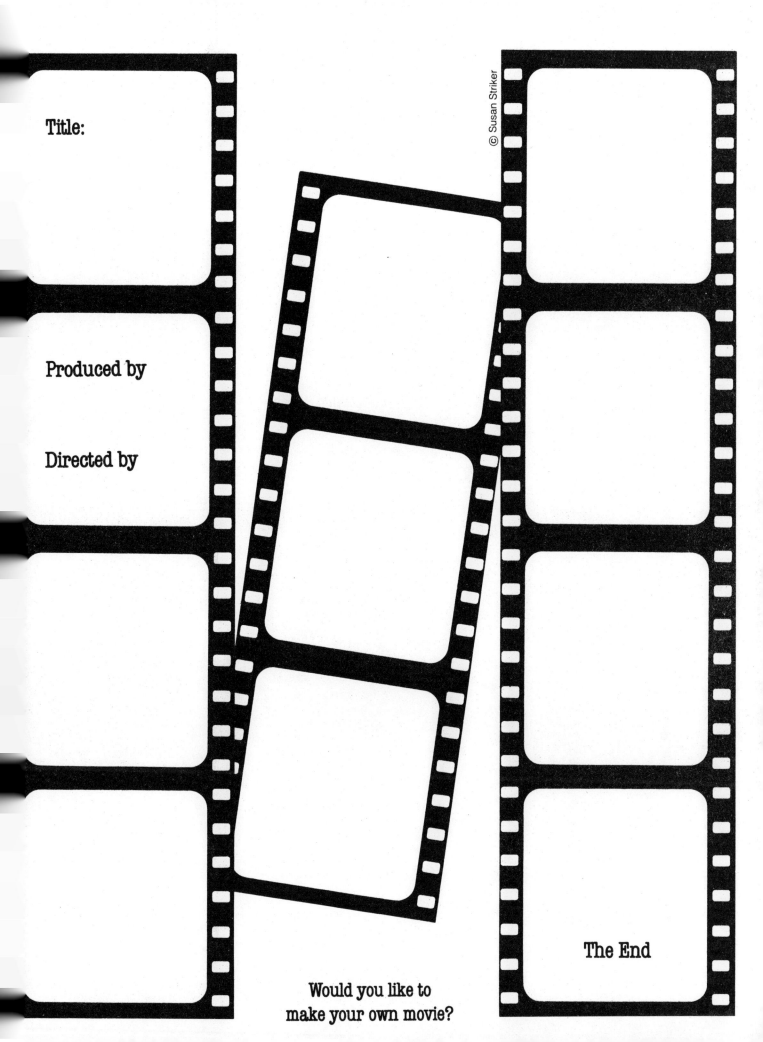

Title:

Produced by

Directed by

The End

Would you like to
make your own movie?

© Susan Striker

What is the worst thing a dragon might do?

© Susan Striker

Can you turn this leaf into something completely different?

Good Friend Award

Awarded to _____

For _____

_____

What would someone have to do to earn this award from you?

eet

are

Have you ever had a dream come true?

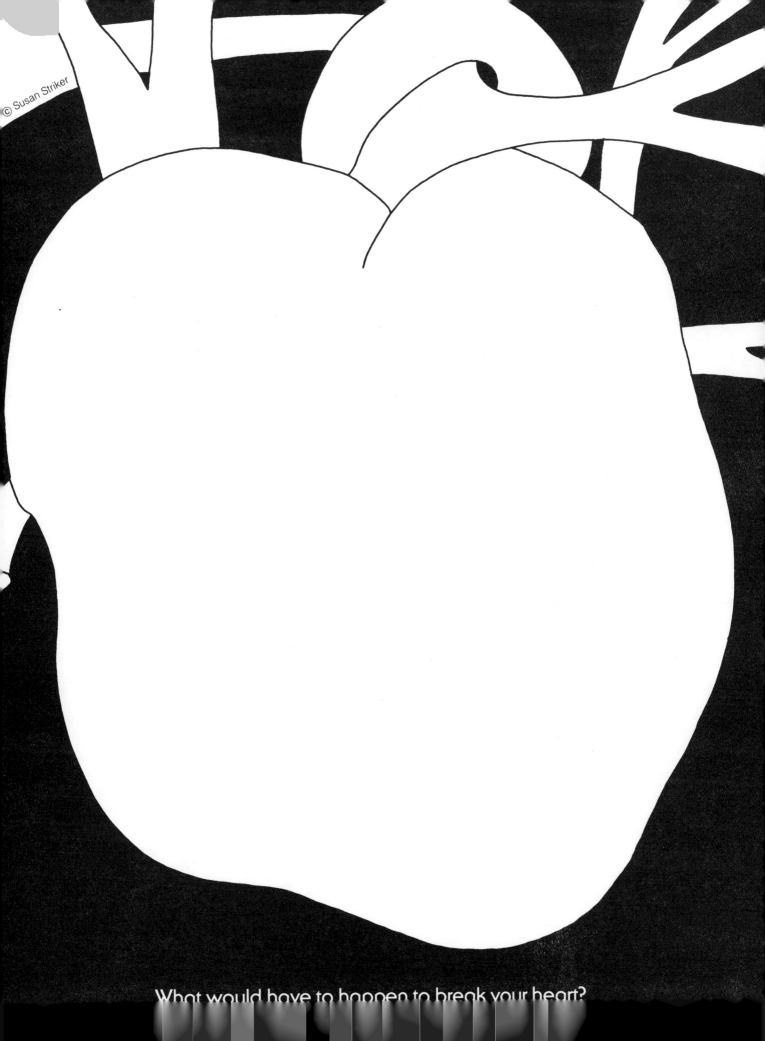

What would have to happen to break your heart?

What has the ship's captain sighted?

If your family moved, where would you want to go?

START

WIN!

Treasure
Hunt
Game

Design your own board game.

What do you daydream about?

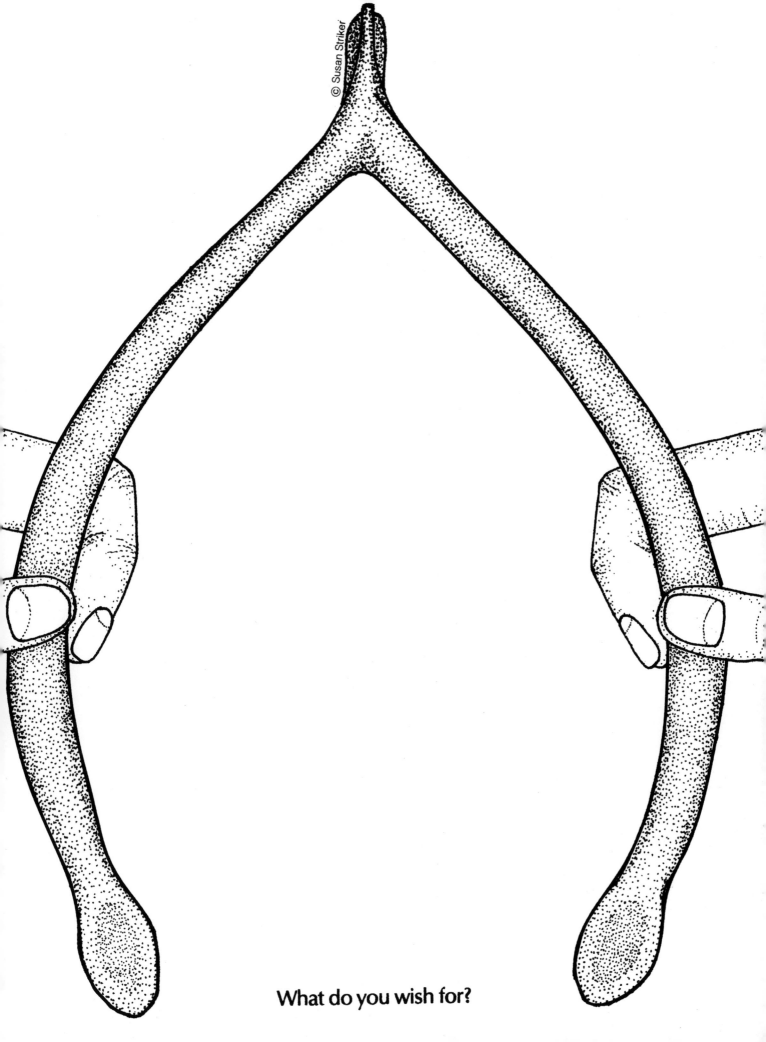

© Susan Striker

What do you wish for?

What amazing tale does this parrot have to tell?

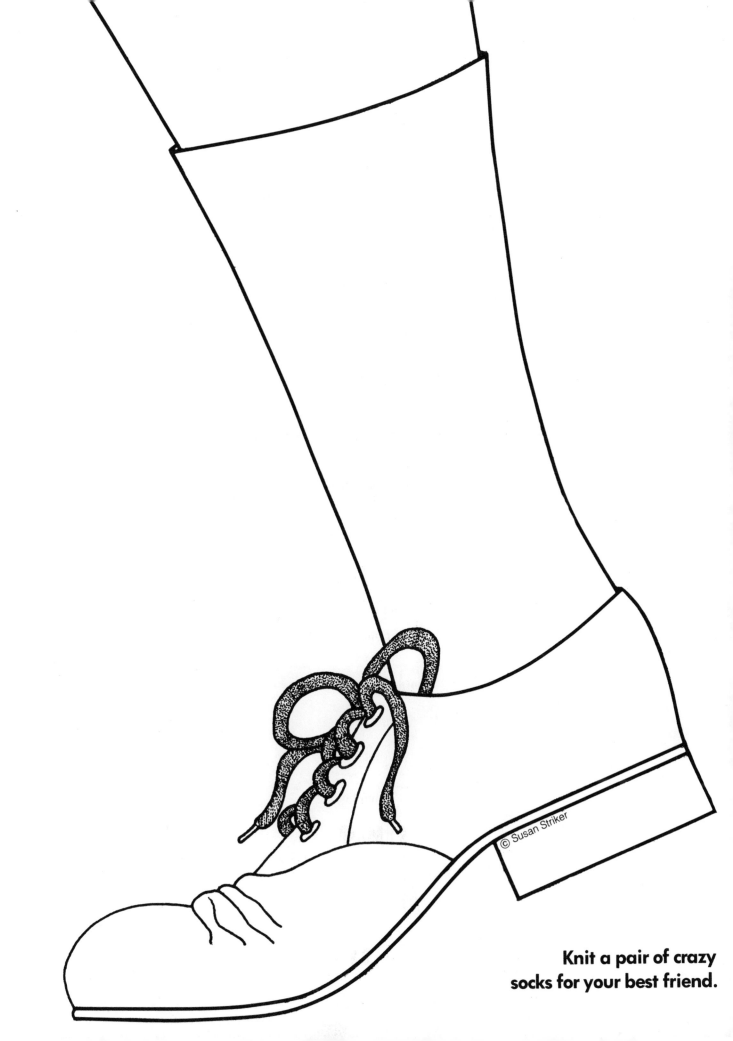

Knit a pair of crazy socks for your best friend.

© Susan Striker

© Susan Striker

This car can go back in time.
Where would you like to go in it?

Design a billboard to discourage people from smoking.

© Susan Striker

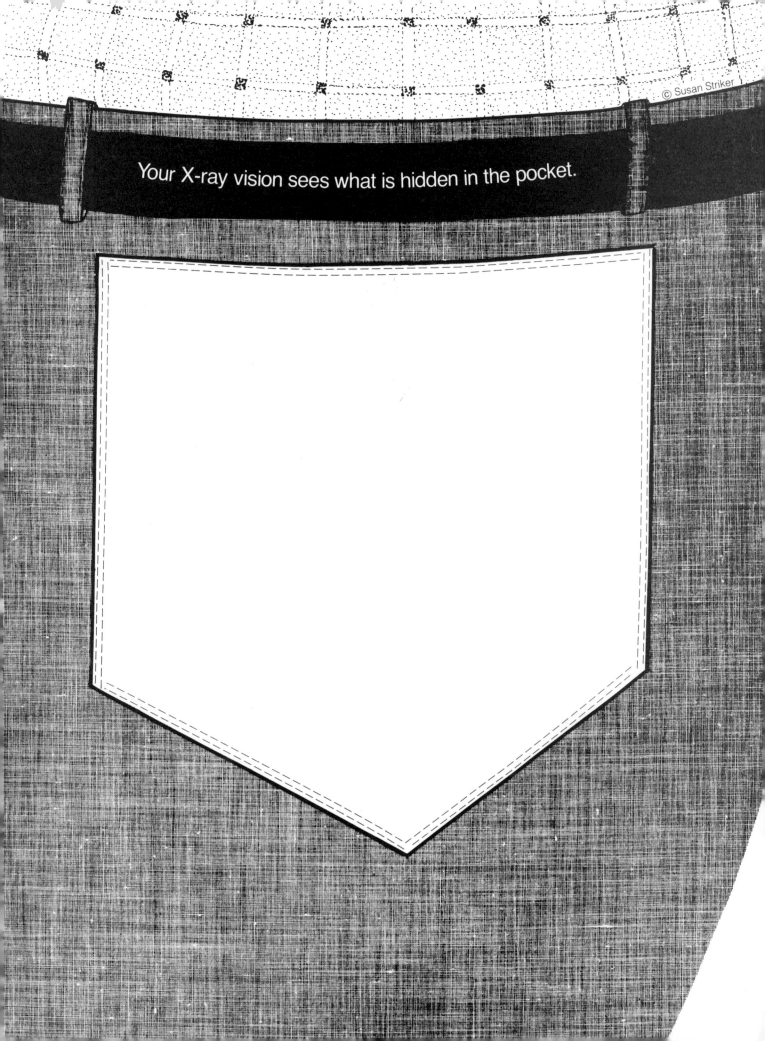

Your X-ray vision sees what is hidden in the pocket.

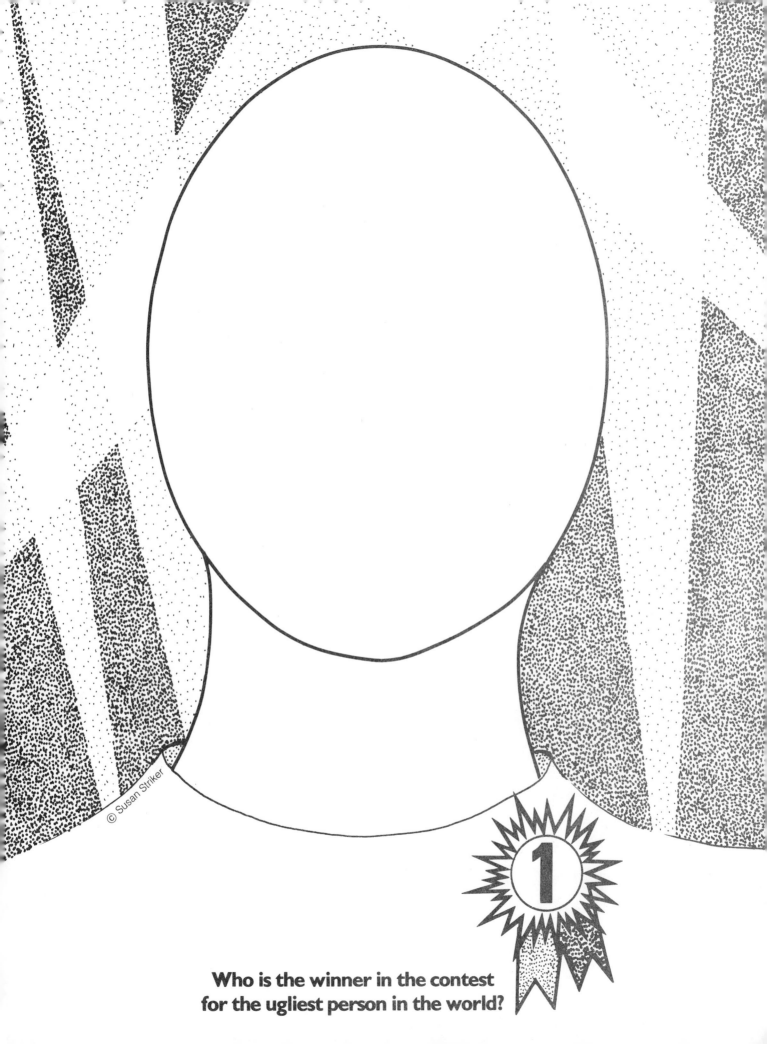

**Who is the winner in the contest
for the ugliest person in the world?**

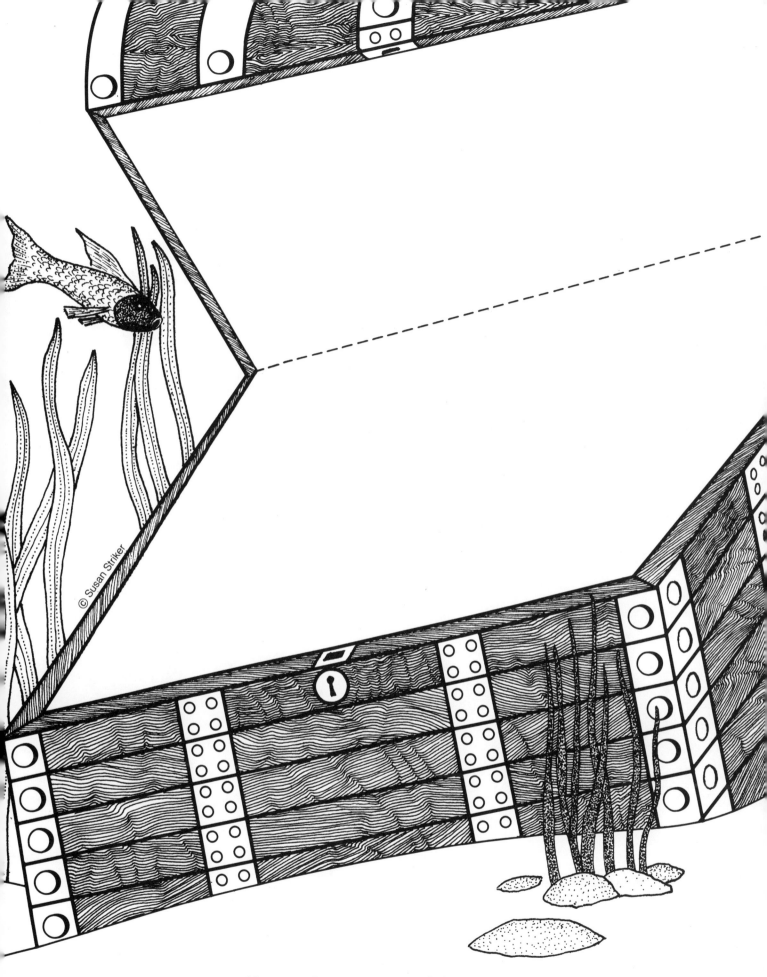

You and your team of divers
just discovered buried treasure.

What kind of pictures do you like to see?

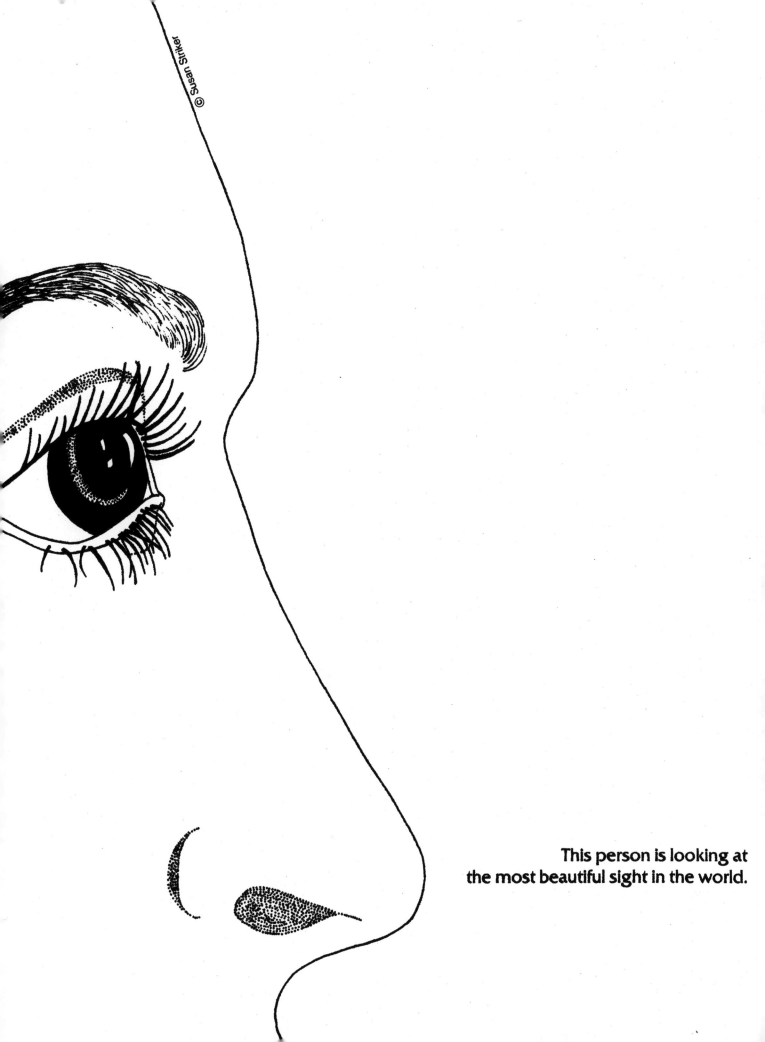

This person is looking at
the most beautiful sight in the world.

THE ANTI COLORING BOOKS®

A complete list.

The Anti-Coloring Book® by Susan Striker and Edward Kimmel
General interest, for ages 6 and older.
ISBN 0-8050-0246-4

The Second Anti-Coloring Book® by Susan Striker with Edward Kimmel
General interest, for ages 6 and older.
ISBN 0-8050-0771-7

The Third Anti-Coloring Book® by Susan Striker
General interest, for ages 6 and older.
ISBN 0-8050-1447-0

The Fourth Anti-Coloring Book® by Susan Striker
General interest, for ages 6 and older.
ISBN 0-8050-2000-4

The Fifth Anti-Coloring Book® by Susan Striker
General interest, for ages 6 and older.
ISBN 0-8050-2376-3

The Sixth Anti-Coloring Book® by Susan Striker
General interest, for ages 6 and older.
ISBN 0-8050-0873-X

The Anti-Coloring Book® of Exploring Space on Earth by Susan Striker
Architecture and interior design.
ISBN 0-8050-1446-2

The Anti-Coloring Book® of Masterpieces by Susan Striker
The world's great art, including color reproductions.
ISBN 0-8050-2644-4

The Inventor's Anti-Coloring Book® by Susan Striker
Inventions, devices, and contraptions.
ISBN 0-8050-2615-0

The Mystery Anti-Coloring Book® by Susan Striker
Mysteries, discoveries, and cops and robbers.
ISBN 0-8050-1600-7

The Newspaper Anti-Coloring Book® by Susan Striker
Write and illustrate your own newspaper.
ISBN 0-8050-1599-X

Look for these at your local bookstore.